BOOK OF WAR

KP
Kassala Publishing

Published by Kassala Publishing in 2009
info@kassala.co.uk

Printed in Great Britain by the MPG Books Group, Bodmin
and King's Lynn.

ISBN 978-0-9563404-0-5

With special thanks to Harry Cummins (editor), David Taylor,
Charles Winter, James Hurley, Andrew Cumming, Ashton
Radcliffe (photographer), Gavin Ingham Brooke, Antonia
Bristowe, David Key, Mary Long, René Carayol, Oonagh
Connolly (designer).

BOOK OF WAR

John Jeffcock

John Jeffcock was born in 1968 in London and spent his early years being educated by Benedictine Monks at Worth Abbey. In 1989 he passed out of the Royal Military Academy Sandhurst to join the Coldstream Guards.

He was part of the Allied Force that entered Iraq and freed Kuwait, the UN protection force in Bosnia-Herzegovina, and served in South Armagh's 'Bandit Country', one of the most notorious parts of Northern Ireland. Over the same period he trained in armoured infantry in Germany, desert and jungle warfare in Kenya and ceremonial duties in London. He was mentioned in despatches, won one of the most arduous infantry competitions and left the army after six years as a captain.

He has master degrees in Business and Poetry and is now Chief Executive of Winmark Limited. He is married to Katrin and lives in London.

Table of contents

Foreword   9

HOME

My Teachers are Proud 13

Believe Me 15

Two Boxes 17

My Death is Planned 19

IRAQ

They Were Going Home 23

Daisy Cutters 25

A State of Mind 27

Sound of Life 29

Defiance 31

Elegantly Sufficient 33

Interrogation 35

Fire Power 37

Arabian Nights 39

NORTHERN IRELAND

Long Range Patrol 43

Fear 45

Belfast Outsiders 47

Surrounded 49

BOSNIA

Letter from Sarajevo 53

What we did 55

UN Target 57

Contact 59

Case Vac 61

Bosnian Roulette 63

Christmas Eve 65

Goražde Force 67

Prepare to Move 69

Blockbusting S1 71

Armed Conflict 73

COMING HOME

Claret 77

Slowly they tell 79

Chelsea Pensioners 81

Soul Riskers 85

Naked 87

Dedication 91

Foreword

These highly personal reminiscences evoke powerful images of war and peace. They demonstrate once again that although war is necessarily brutal, soldiers nevertheless are humans who are able to think about moral issues and who can also sympathize with the predicament of their fellow beings. John Jeffcock's collection of poems makes a valuable addition to the modern literature of war.

General Sir Michael Rose KCB CBE DSO QGM DL

HOME

My Teachers are Proud

I sit confused by my education, bemused by degrees
I was taught biology but I cannot heal
I learnt sociology but know nothing of educating a family
I have studied the laws of physics but still cannot
manage my own time
I have experimented in chemistry but am shy
with strangers
I have learnt a thousand dates but fail in relationships
I can remember the equation of a circle but not how
to judge a group
I was taught religion but not how to help a vagrant
I am trained in violence
And my teachers are proud

Believe Me

Believe me when I say it's true, that we were scared
Trust me that when we laughed at death we did not lose
respect
Have faith that in the time of need we will not fail
Have hope as this is earth on which we walk
Have charity on what we do in haste
Humanity on those whose fate we hold
Seize me as you would the day, if what we do is wrong
Love me as this is why we bear the weight

Two Boxes

In a room packed up and bare
A mother and two boxes
One for the army
One with her name
Stamped on three sides

Her son stands beside her
The author of the letter
In the box for his mother
That neither one wants read.

An uncomfortable goodbye
A few rehearsed words
A mother pregnant with tears
A face of failing composure.

In a warehouse nearby
Full of letters unwanted
Is a mountain of disastrous boxes
Being eroded away

My Death is Planned

My letter is written
My box is packed
My next of kin is filed
My death is planned

The "Families Officer", the appointed Ambassador
of Death
Starched from cap to boots
Rehearses the briefest of bad tidings
For the waiting next of kin
And from its special drawer
Comes canned condolence
As swift as does the pressed and ever pristine coffin flag
The posthumous award
Shines like the ferryman's coin

"The regiment will look after you now"

IRAQ

They Were Going Home

Under one week later
The battalion as a convoy
Was filing down the road to Basra in Iraq.

"Death Alley"
A gorge fenced in on either side
By cliffs of obliterated vehicles
Each one still packed with blackened naked men.

A fleeing army heading home
Straffed, napalmed and "transported" beyond
recognition.
Bulldozed into heaps in the name of efficiency.
Brave men commanded now by rabid dogs
Who come to scavenge in a locust swarm.

Twenty kilometres of hope
And each was silenced.

Forty minutes it took to pass
Some slept and never saw it.
Some looked but were entranced by burning oil wells
and the blackened sky
Some ate, because they were hungry.

Daisy Cutters

We were not warned of this attack
We did not see the vapour trails of planes
Or hear the hellish siren of the shrieking load
Or know the target –
How far from us the Daisy Cutters fell

The ground around us did not merely shake
It lurched in pain
The gridnet of the target-maker's map
Dissected our adversary like lamb
Melted his troops like snowmen in a forest fire

Tomorrow is G+3
When we must cross the Rubicon of War
Tonight the stars jump down and wreck the Earth
Like Samson, blinded, or the fatal asteroids
That bring destruction to the worlds that will not change
It was tonight the Daisy Cutters fell

And we the soldiers that these cannibals protect
Feel brother only to their victims
Our fellow artists in the trade of War
Who took our place like virgins in the Dance of Death
Thank God, this time, the Earth has moved for them
and not for us.

A State of Mind

G + 1
10km short of the Iraqi border
1 UK Divisional Assembly Area
Night

Soldiers sleep with eyes wide open, waiting for the
order to move
The incessant grumble of artillery mutters on
And the convoy of tanks that has been passing us for
the last two days
Becomes an armoured caravan of shells
That cuts through the highway like a steel flood

A signal comes through
"The airmen have been beaten to death"
No one says a thing
What need is there?
A soldier shakes his head
As if to free it from the public stocks
The tingling razor of reality

The present becomes all-excluding
The brain electrifies, a tripwire sensitive to foreign dust
And those we love, distractions now like flies
Burn up inside the everlasting "now"
The lamp of War, at which we charge like moths

The eyes of soldiers lock on targets like a circling hawk's
And yet, up close, seem lost and shallow, like a wolf's
Logic hunts, machine becomes man, love cremated

Sound of Life

No shadow leapt up from behind him
No majestic light fell from the sky
No magical power passed from inside him
No histrionic tension filled the air

No cry left his lips
Just a muted thud
As his body crumbled to the ground
Unbearable thud
Not loud enough, not noble enough, not anything
Enough

I saw it
There was really something there
A giant like the statue of a life
Now there is nothing
Just a banal thud
Growing fainter as it trembles.

Defiance

They stand, defiance in their eyes
The fear of pain has lost its magic hold
We have more prisoners than ammunition
And they have done their maths
We cannot kill them all

Suddenly it swings, and now we are the threatened
Safety catches off, rifles raised, elbows tightened
We give our final warnings
Nothing changes
Ringleaders are targeted
We turn on them like cornered wolves

Negotiations have failed
Now they are nearer the end of our rifles than we are
The last excruciating pause
As our eyes move to the gunsights

Their leaders freeze, and then, like ice, they break
Again the spirit moves the Ouija Board
The eyes of the Iraqis drop like sheep's
They fall upon the ground like patient kids
Our rifles fall. The tension bursts like Spring.

Elegantly Sufficient

In Sarajevo we tried to feed the women
They were hungry but would not eat
It was two weeks before we asked them why
Before we gave them rations to take home
Their families were starving

In the Gulf we collected food
From the trenches for the prisoners
Gave it to the officers to distribute to the other ranks.
They shared nothing
And ate it in front of their men
On whose shoulders they had gained promotion

Interrogation

Frightened soldiers smell, prisoners radiate
A beggar's bouquet, the cologne of war
But this was not all we found when we searched
Hoarders of dried prunes, the rust of home and
devalued banknotes

They were survivors, deflowered by artillery barrage,
marked men.
They had surrendered, shaking and confused
We offered them no peace

We separate the officers and men
Arrest each man with freshly-issued boots
Place them in a stress position
Patrol the lines
Baton everyone's mistakes

They arrive in shock, the interrogator's weapon
We, his armourer, keep them disorientated
Whilst stunned, they will betray
Our window of opportunity

The war is not yet won
Time is life.

Fire Power

Three divisions of Republican Guard
97% battle effective
A thousand armoured vehicles
Five thousand fighting men

Thirty-six squadrons of Apache helicopters
Attack speed
One hundred seconds

Three divisions of Republican Guard
2% battle effective
Twenty armoured vehicles
Two hundred fighting men

Arabian Nights

Seized and searched, stripped
Intimately exposed to a defeated enemy
The object of a pathological revenge
Bludgeoned by fists

In a room without exits, without taboos, without sleep,
without time, without clemency

He chants his name, rank, number
Clinging to roots like torn trees in a hurricane
Retreating to his inner place, the hidden self
Parched, he prays in hymns, the names of loved ones,
songs from childhood
Still the intruders strike, leaving no sanctuary

This hour was the hour of the paper towels
Each one was stuffed right down his back
Ignited

Broken both inside and through skin
Survival is not what he longs for
Just peace, in unconsciousness

NORTHER IRELAND
South Armagh

Long Range Patrol

Our shoulders freeze under the weight
Our eyes squint past the rivers of dried sweat
That streak our bodies.
Lips break like crackling, skin rubs to yeasty paste
All fat on the soles of our feet is burnt
We walk on muscle

The hardest men are faltering
Raging tempers, barely hidden
As the patrol spreads and slows
Rank clashes with rank.

We can fight pain
But sleep is breaking us

Fear

Some soldiers will not aim at the enemy
Some cannot stand when under fire
Some risk everything for a stranger
Others celebrate the day they were injured
None are cowards

Some soldiers will not take responsibility
Some will never volunteer
Some lose themselves for a fool
Others break before the fight has begun
None are cowards

There is only wisdom in fear
Love in bravery
Death in killing

Belfast Outsiders

Another tired car cruises down the straights
In botanical shirts, they smoke leaves
Their long hair brushes past shops
They stop short, at the lights
They stop too short

The car does not belch, it purrs
A flick of hair shows trained eyes
Young men, fit in face, too clean
Unmarked car at the lights

Ghosts in the straights
Men with pistol engraved thighs
Like insects in the urban foliage
Suddenly spotted
Before fading from view

Surrounded

He spat and smiled: "We got one of you bastards last
night"
He was mistaken, they got more than one.
They got his wife, twenty four
Married just three months before the tour
They got his mother, his father, they got his sisters
They got his school and boyhood friends from home.
They got his platoon and the men he had trained.
They got his mates and the men he had fought with.

Four of those mates stood close beside the killer
On a witness empty street
Trained and armed, jury and judge
Not needing an excuse

They glanced at each other
Finished the search
And simply walked away

BOSNIA
United Nations
Protection Force

Letter from Sarajevo

Sarajevo, FRY, BFPO 547   7 April 1994

Dear David
Vesna was shot going home by the Serbs last night
– her own people! The round went through her leg and
fortunately missed both bone and artery. We managed
to get her to hospital OK and she'll be fine but she'll
probably limp for a while.

She has had a strange life – air hostess / model / TV
presenter and now our interpreter. A Serb married
to a Muslim, in a country torn apart by religion, yet she
manages to hold the whole thing together. We need more
of her, we all need more of her.

She laughed when we went to see her, the Serbs had just
sent her flowers, then we appear with army chocolate.
She told me how it all started, how a barricade appeared
one day as she drove to work and how she took an
alternative route. The next day all the routes were
blocked so she called work and said she couldn't come in.
Then someone shot somebody from a different religion
and it all kicked off.

David she looked pretty bad. I think her family has been
ostracised by both communities and is going to be in
trouble without us. The tour ends in six weeks and we will
do what we can but I cannot let her become dependent .
We all know the score.

Keep your head down.
Yours J

What we did

We held guns at the heads of children
Stealing equipment off our vehicles
And they gave us the finger

We filled the bunkers
That other soldiers fled from
To hide from artillery

We scooped villagers off the roads
And dumped them in the freezing river
For blocking the convoy routes

We found the mass graves
And laid out the bodies
For their families to identify

We set standards that kept people alive
Yet negotiated with war criminals
To ensure aid to communities

We defended the vehicles
That they turned their artillery pieces on
When they saw the air strike reconnaissance

We destroyed their bunkers
Occupied by their soldiers
Fed by our aid

We knew each faction would lie
Yet we trusted our interpreters
More than our national press

UN Target

Army boxer
Born in Newcastle
Married, three daughters
London Division heavyweight champion

Sarajevo
Showing a young family his armoured UN vehicle
A treat for their three daughters
He smiles sagely at the father
Giving hope where all is bitterness
A tower of life where nothing lives
He cradles the youngest like his own

Then it struck
First the brilliant white
Then the pressure wave
Pulsing with hornet swarms of spinning shot
A blast that spat out eardrums
Fragments
Then the whistling hum of driving hail
Nature inverted
Shrapnel
Debris

The family like sodden wrapping paper
Were shredded in his arms
But he survived, untouched
The UN Target.
Revenge, a lesson that must not be learnt.

Contact

Hello Zero Alpha this is Echo One Zero Alpha over
Her soft golden hair gently veils my face
Zero Alpha send over
Her warm full chest lies rising on mine
Echo One Zero Alpha contact Grid 756438 – Call sign
Bravo under effective fire – request Hotel Two Zero over
Her knees brace my body sure and straight
Zero Alpha out to you – Hello Hotel Two Zero over
And her feet cup the back of my thighs
Hotel Two Zero I acknowledge Echo One Zero Alpha's last
– you have figures nine minutes over
Her framed head tilts slightly
Roger – out to you – Echo One Zero Alpha you have
figures
four minutes over
Her whole face shines and smiles
Hello Hotel Two Zero this is Echo One Zero Alpha –
fire mission over
No words are spoken
Hotel Two Zero send over
But the silence is swiftly read
Echo One Zero Alpha fire mission Grid 757441 over
Sense and movement belong alone to her
Hotel Two Zero I read back Grid 757441 over
I am beautifully disarmed
Echo One Zero Alpha correct over
Grateful to my captor
Hotel Two Zero watch my fire – wait – wait – wait – over
I have returned whence I came
Echo One Zero Alpha on target – fire for effect – out

Casevac

Hello Zero Alpha this is Zero Bravo casevac
EC Monitoring vehicle broke our check point
Vehicle hit mine on route steel at time 08.51 hours
Two Two Charlie en route to assist slid off route into
minefield
Casualties in both call signs
Request casevac over

Zero Alpha negative
Airspace is closed
Tell your callsigns to move to protect the down callsigns
Out to you

Hello all callsigns this is Zero Alpha
Air strikes in figures five
Prepare for strike retaliations
Two Zero Alpha acknowledge over

Two Zero Alpha roger out

Bosnian Roulette

She would wake praying in her prison
Every morning before the first light
Kneeling well back from the shell hole, the sniper's bullseye
in the shattered wall
That took her like a telescope toward her family home

She could just see their innocent faces
Mouthing "Mummy, we miss you"
Daddy holding them back.
She counted each obsessively
By name, by name, by name, by name, by name
Five, they are safe, thank God, there are still five.

But darkness injured her
For Night with its every amplified sound
Came like the click of a safety catch
It jumped on Day like Death
Playing Russian Roulette with her children

All that lay between them was the distance of a football pitch
A stone's throw
A short sprint
For there were no bars, no walls, no wire, no fences
Just the relentless aim
Of the snipers who never slept
The wardens of her cell

Christmas Eve

We'll be live on the 10 o'clock news
In two minutes time, singing hymns
In a gym that no one knew existed
Too many of us encased by one room
Helmets off, body armour on, rifles slung.

A fire fight rattles nearer
The chaplain signals to sing louder
"Silent Night" is cut short
But "Hark the Herald Angels sing" roars up like "Men
of Harlech" from a pit-head choir.
The crackle of gunfire is winning.

An invisible nod
Sergeants cut through the back
Section commanders disappear
Camp defenders stand to.

The front ranks hold
The camera rolls
The reality of location remains firmly hidden
The singing becomes clinical
As our minds rehearse the drill.

The room shudders
The camera cuts the shot.
The volume goes to max
As six hundred boots stamp out of the corridors

Goražde Force

The UN guarantees another enclave
But no more men

Orders are given, we wait
Forces are split, sleep halves
Then halves again

Notice periods disappear, reappear, disappear, reappear
Unpack, pack, unpack, pack, unpack, pack

Two weeks sitting on helmets
Waiting on politicians
Sitting on helmets
Waiting on politicians
Sitting on helmets
Waiting on politicians

Cold rations, no washing, cold rations, no washing
Sitting on helmets
Waiting on politicians
Sitting on helmets
Waiting on politicians

Sleep halves, then halves again
Forces are split, orders are given

But no more men
The UN guarantees another enclave

Prepare to Move

The Mujahideen are sweeping down the valley
Killing everything in their path
Every sense is savaged by their approach

UN soldiers rush back to vehicles
Engines roar, antennas power-up, weapons are armed
The order is given, the UN is leaving.
Men fall on their knees
And beg 'take my child'
The women lay their new born
Under the track of the vehicles.

Soldiers refuse to drive
Court martials are threatened
The tracks roll.

The women dive and save their children
But our tracks would have been kinder
Than what befell them on the following day
The next village was bigger
And we could not protect them both

Blockbusting S1

In a warm tunnel of diesel
A corridor of UN armour
Stops short, within range
It dominates the field.
Our faces are masked by technology
Our jaws are locked like frozen gears
Our ears are warmed by radios
The brine that bathes our eyes has frosted like a cataract.
Patience is ebbing.

We glimpse Serb tanks between the trees
Their purple combat jackets restrain their lunging dogs
That guard a single roadblock
The checkpoint that chokes off the Aid.

UN negotiators exposed between walls of armour
Call in favours
As soldiers glance at soldiers
Weighing judging dreading

But the whine of UN jets
Breaks Serbian pride
As their fragile egos shudder
Against an overwhelming force

Saving face they impose conditions
They search our vehicles looking for pride
Finding only porn, they win a moral victory
The roadblock seems to matter little now.

The bar lifts
The Aid rolls
The people live

Armed Conflict

They shot our interpreters as they stood next to us
They stole fuel from our camps
They surrounded soldiers with civilians then took our weapons
They cut supplies to negotiate for aid
They mined our path
They executed people under our protection
They targeted our vehicles
They shelled our camps
They kidnapped charity workers
They played nations off against each other
They killed us and our replacements

COMING HOME

Claret

Four bottles of his favourite claret
It took
Before he talked

He had been through the numbness
The nervous laughter at death
The internal isolation from reality
The self-imposed exile from his fellow man

He was bored
Bored of being matted in another person's blood
Bored of picking up fragments of comrades he had
trained
Bored of meeting civilians whose pampered lives he
couldn't comprehend
Bored of his reality

He needed to come home
To heal.
But there were no tickets
All routes were closed

Slowly they tell

Loving wives prepare homes
Others prepare confessions
They embrace as lovers
But meet as strangers

Husbands have changed
Are present but have not returned
They fumble at domestic etiquette
Find emptiness in normality
Casual release in unplanned cruelty

Lost in the arms of loved ones
Soldiers are drawn back to soldiers
Wives mourn when they should rescue
Husbands drink when they should confess.

Chelsea Pensioners

They came in red
And lined the barracks
To watch the corps of drums

The corps in red
Marched bearskin high
To the single beat of the drum

To the left and right
They passed in lines
Until the thunder of their drums

Shook you
Like the distant thunder
Of artillery

From the left
The pensioners started to sing
Until in unison
The voices reached out
They remembered

One cried
He had remembered
What?
He would not say
It does not matter
He had remembered

The last post was played
We all stood to attention
Silence
The single bugler
Silence

Soul Riskers

Old soldiers confess
The deeds that cannot be undone
Accepting the order that cannot be changed

They fear not their death
Nor pain nor the wearing of bones
But the questions they will be asked

They fought for love
The love of their people and kinsmen
Whose needs outweighed their survival

Now their individual choices must be weighed
The causes and the people are gone
And the scales of justice draw near

They did not know what they risked
But they bear its enormous weight
Forgiveness is all they ask

Naked

I want to walk in your dreams
To see what you ache for
To touch the centre of your sorrow
And show you the beauty that I see in you

I want us to live in a world without walls
To be who we aspire to be together
To be giants in our own company
And to give knowing that what we have is enough

I want to stand naked next to your true self
To be proud of all you are
To question not your faith nor doubt your word
And when all is lost, walk with you through the fire

John Jeffcock

This book is dedicated to all those who deploy on active service and the friends and families who support.

Army Benevolent Fund

As the demand on the Army continues to remain high, so do the needs of serving and former soldiers. The call on help from the Army Benevolent Fund has never been higher and is predicted to keep rising.

During the last year the Soldiers' Charity provided assistance to over 3,100 people; a rise of 20% and a record total of £2.5 million in grants was given to individuals. Our total expenditure was £6.5 million of which £4 million was voluntary income.

Mobility and debt have been by far the biggest calls for assistance, clearly reflecting the current economic climate and the impact of current operations. Cases like Trooper Shine, a 25-year-old serving with the 2nd Battalion the Royal Tank Regiment who lost his leg when the tank he was driving hit a roadside bomb. The Army Benevolent Fund provided funds to allow his mother to build a walk-in shower in her house so he no longer has to strip wash in the bathroom.

Or Steve Gill. He lost both legs and an eye when patrolling the Falls Road in 1989, but his determination has ensured that he leads an energetic and full life. The ABF provided him with a specialised wheelchair which allows him to participate in wheelchair basketball. Steve also visits the lads at Selly Oak, helping them come to terms with their injuries and encouraging them to keep going and not give up.

These people never look for an easy handout and have frequently lived with great hardship before they consider asking for help. But when they do the Army Benevolent Fund is there, just as we are there for any soldier – current or ex-serving – and their families.

www.armybenfund.org